Not Every Dollar

John Lemmon

Not Every Dollar Is Equal by John Lemmon

Copyright © 2017, 2019 John Lemmon

All rights reserved. No portion of this book may be reproduced in any form without permission from the author/publisher, except as permitted by Australian copyright law. For permissions contact the author at: jlemmon1153@gmail.com

ISBN: 9781694406088

DISCLAIMER

Some parts of this book are fictional. Names, characters, places, and incidents are entirely the products of the author's imagination. Any resemblance to actual persons, living or dead, businesses, companies, events, or locales is entirely coincidental. Where any true stories have been included, the names, identities and locations of the persons and/or companies involved have been changed to protect their privacy.

I am not a lawyer or a practicing accountant. The content provided herein is simply for educational purposes and does not take the place of legal advice from your lawyer or financial advice from your accountant. Every effort has been made to ensure that the content provided in this book is accurate and helpful for readers at publishing time. However, this is not an exhaustive treatment of the subject. No liability is assumed for losses or damages due to the information provided. You are responsible for your own choices, actions, and results. You should consult your lawyer and accountant for your specific legal, financial and other questions and needs.

Table of Contents

Introduction 3
The Story of Joe 6
Why Businesses Go Broke 10
What Is Profit? 12
Goals 15
It's Not How Much You Get, It's How Much You Get To Keep 18
The See-Saw Is Better Than The Swing 21
Not Every Dollar Is Equal 27
The Power Of One Dollar 38
No Pain, No Gain 45
The Discounting Dilemma 53
Summary 66

Introduction

This book is intended to help businesses gain a better understand of the pricing and cost control decisions they make, especially in relation to how these decisions affect the business profitability.

Pricing is a key component for any business to ensure they make profits that will sustain the business and achieve the business goals. Every business needs money to achieve their goals, and there are a number of ways to get the money they need. The purpose of this book is to look at some of the methods available to maximize profitability primarily through pricing and costing decisions, so that business owners and managers can better understand and utilize these principles to positively impact their business.

This book is for…

- Small business owners and business managers

- Sales people who are negotiating prices

- Retail shops where discounts are often offered over the counter

- Large businesses that employ sales people

- Accountants and managers who need to educate their sales staff

- Anyone involved in the pricing and profitability processes of the business

Let me start by saying, nothing in this book is rocket science. It is all very simple and will be obvious to many readers once they read it. Any readers who are accountants will see immediately what I am driving at. But even the accountants may learn something, even if it is only to pass the information on to the sales and marketing team so they "get it."

Like many really simple concepts, sometimes things can be overlooked. In the case of pricing and the impact on profitability, business people often overlook the depth of detail in this information, and do so at their own peril. As has often been said, "Common sense is often not that common."

It doesn't really matter what size or type of business you are in. The information is just as relevant to sole traders, partnerships, small enterprises and right through to major corporations. Likewise, it is relevant to retail, manufacturing, wholesale and service based businesses, including those both online and offline.

Every form of business is affected by pricing decisions because pricing, along with costing, impacts profitability.

How this book came about

Some years ago I was working for a major industrial products company as their Business Support / Commercial Manager.

The sales department for one of the regions was holding a conference to discuss strategy and paths going forward. It was my role to present sales results and targets for the coming period.

That day I was also asked to present some other information, but was unable to do so as we were waiting on agreement from the corporate legal team before presenting it. Unfortunately the legal people did not come through in time, so I had 15-20 minutes to fill. The filler I created was a short presentation on pricing that really struck a chord with the audience, more so even than the "real" presentation.

I had numerous people come to me, both on that day and in the weeks and months that followed, saying they had never realized the impact of their pricing decisions and what it meant to the bottom line. Later, I was also asked to update the presentation and give it to other audiences in the retail chain network to address some of the "less than satisfactory" pricing decisions they were making.

In the months that followed I was approached by the national sales training center for the business asking if they could include my presentation as part of the regular training in Commercial Best Practice. I also received a call from the Global Commercial team asking if it could be included in the Global Sales and Commercial training packages.

I later discovered that the presentation (somehow) leaked out into another major national Telecommunications organization and was being rolled out there.

Not bad for a quick throwaway filler presentation!

Given that so many people found this information to be of value in their line of business, I thought it would be valuable to share it with anyone who is interested…and thus this book came to be.

Structure of this book

Unfortunately, this stuff (you know…accounting…yawn!) can be pretty darned dry. I don't want you using it as a surefire cure for insomnia as you read it. (That still might happen anyway…but think of the cost savings you'll make on sleeping tablets if it does! Ha!)

So I have used a fictional story as the vehicle for driving the book forward to present the information in a way that I hope will:

1. Link the elements together in a logical sequence

2. Show how the information actually works using simple examples

3. Be interesting and entertaining (…and keep you awake!)

In a few places I have included real stories of actual events I have personally seen or experienced in my business life, and these are indicated in the text of the book with the words 'true story.' All of the things I have written about are based on true experiences and lessons learned, either from mistakes made or observed, or learned from people I know and respect. The use of the 'story-telling' mode just helps to convey the message in a way that can relate to a specific business, (indeed it could be any business), without relying solely on dry academic models. I hope you find this method helpful.

So without further ado, let me introduce you to "Joe" who has a small barbershop business and is having a few struggles…

The Story of Joe

This is the story of Joe.

Joe runs a small business in a local shopping strip. He is a men's barber and he has been running his shop for a number of years.

Joe is doing OK, but he wants and needs to earn some more money. His family is growing up and he has to pay for the wedding expenses of two grown daughters in the next year or two.

I walked into his shop one morning to get a haircut. I love going to his shop. There are no appointments, you just take a seat and wait your turn. You can roughly tell how long it will be by the number of people ahead of you.

Joe is great at customer service, and because I've been coming to him for a few years, he always yells out to me as I walk in. "Hey Johnny! Great to see you man. Take a seat and I'll be with you shortly." And then he goes back to the guy whose hair he is cutting and continues his conversation with him.

It's a great atmosphere in Joe's shop. The guys all talk sports and who is going to win some upcoming match, who is doing well and what their plans are for upcoming holidays. The shop has the smell of a good old barbershop too, and guys just feel comfortable there. (No offence meant to the ladies, the information is just as relevant to any business).

After a short wait my turn comes around, so I take a seat in the chair and Joe starts in on my hair.

"So how are things going Joe?" I ask.

"Yeah, well, its a bit up and down. You know my girls are getting married soon so I'm trying to do some things a bit differently to make some extra money," he replies.

"Oh yeah? And how's that going for you?" I ask.

"Well…it's still early days, but I'm hoping for the best. I mean, at present I'm breaking even, but I gotta get a few more dollars to do what I need to do." Joe says.

"I hear ya buddy. Kids can cost you a fortune…and weddings! Don't start me on THAT little expense! I remember what it was like when my daughters got married!" I empathized.

And so the conversation went for the next fifteen minutes until he had finished my cut. As usual Joe did a great job and I happily paid him the twelve bucks for the cut and left his shop.

Some time later when my hair was getting unruly again, I popped into Joe's shop for another cut. "Hey Joe!" I called out as I took my seat. But Joe didn't look his normal cheerful self that day. He looked up at me, nodded without a response, and quietly went back to work on the guy in the chair.

Clearly, something was wrong. Even the atmosphere in the shop seemed strained.

As I looked around the shop I noticed he had another chair in the shop, and just then a guy came out from the back and called the next chap in line to have his hair cut. I thought to myself, "Hmm...seems like Joe is expanding."

Shortly, my turn came and I sat down in the chair with Joe ready to cut my hair.

"How are things Joe? Looks like your building the business up what with the extra chair and all? Who is the new guy?" I said as I took my seat.

Joe sighed and said, "Yeah, that was the plan when I brought Julio on board. I was hoping to make some more money to do the things I need to do with the family, so I thought an extra chair would allow us to do some more cuts and increase the money coming in. But it hasn't quite worked out as well as I thought it would."

"No? Are the customers not coming in?" I asked.

"Well...yeah we are getting more people in the door, and Julio is a really good barber. But at the end of the day I'm just not making the extra money I hoped for." Joe said. "It's all a bit frustrating at present."

"How's that?" I asked.

"Well, to get more people in I thought I'd run some promotions to let people know we had a new guy here. I run a discount offer on Tuesdays to try and get a few more people through the door. We knock 10% off the normal price, but it hasn't made a lot of difference. We have got a few more people coming in, but I'm not seeing the money increase as much as I had hoped."

"I have a pretty good, loyal clientele, so I don't want to do anything that might upset them. I'm getting kinda frustrated and I really don't know what to do!" Joe responded in frustration.

"So let me get this straight," I said. "You have an extra guy here so you can do more cuts and increase your income. You are running some discounts to try and increase the number of cuts each week, but you aren't getting the results you want. Is that pretty much it?"

"Pretty much." He replied.

I felt sorry for Joe. He's a good guy and we have known each other for quite a while. It made me upset to see him in this situation, so I thought I'd offer him a proposition.

"Joe, did you know that I worked in and ran a range of businesses for years, and now that I'm basically retired I consult with business owners to help them sort out problems in their businesses?" I told him.

"Well, yeah. I think you told me that once before. But right now I can't afford to pay anyone to help me out. I just don't really have the money," He said sadly.

"I'll tell you what, how about I come over to your place and have a look at your situation. Maybe I can suggest a few things that will help you get back on your feet. If that works, we can talk about whether you want to retain my services on a more permanent basis. And if I can't help, it won't cost you a thing. What do you reckon?"

"You mean you'd help me out without paying for it?" Joe said in shock! "I can't accept charity!"

"OK, but it's still clear you need help. So how about we get together, look at your business and I can offer some suggestions. If you like it and it helps you resolve your problems, you can pay me my usual fee, but only AFTER we see whether the suggestions help you out. What do you say?" I offered.

"Well…OK. I suppose I've got nothing to lose and everything to gain," Joe said. "Let's do it."

After he finished up my haircut we planned to get together later that week after work, and thus began the journey of discovery for Joe where he really started to understand how his business works…

Why Businesses Go Broke

Joe and I got together one night later that week. Joe was still pretty despondent, and despairing of finding a solution to his problems.

"Joe," I said. "Before we get into the business end of things, let's have a look at some of the general issues facing all businesses. It may help to understand a few other things before we get to the pointy end to look at the issues in your business."

"OK," he said. "Whatever you think is best."

"Joe, do you know why most businesses go broke?" I asked.

"Well I guess there could be a lot of reasons," he said.

"You're right," I replied, "They go broke for a whole bunch of reasons. They lose a key market, a key person in a small business dies or takes ill, they suffer litigation, they run out of money, they over-capitalize, they grow too fast and can't keep up, they lose a major contract, and so on. But what do you think the number one reason might be?"

Joe replied, "Well I don't really know for sure, but I guess it would have to do with money, or more likely the lack of it. I mean, most of those things you just mentioned have to do with money shortages in one form or another don't they?"

"That's right Joe. At the lowest common denominator in most business failures you can track the prime issue back to money problems. I once was told that of all the small businesses that open up in any given year, some 75%-80% would close their doors within the next five years, and the primary reason for those failures comes down to poor money management." I responded.

"So you think my problems are poor money management?" Joe asked indignantly.

"No, Joe. Not at all. You have been in business for quite a long time and you are pretty good with managing your money. You pay your wages, suppliers, taxes, and so on without too much difficulty. You are careful with what you get, plus you have survived a couple of recessions." I said.

"Yeah, that's right!" he brightened up. "Even in a recession people still need their hair cut!"

We had a bit of a chuckle over that, but he was right.

"So if my money management is OK, why am I having these difficulties and what can I do to improve my lot?" He questioned.

"The reason I brought up the issue of how businesses go

bust is so that you will understand how fragile business really is. There are no guarantees of success, which is why you need to take the time to read the economic environment and act accordingly." I said. "The economy is always changing. It is never static, and you need to understand what might affect your business and then take steps to minimize the impact of any external economic and environmental issues, if you can."

"What kind of things?" he asked.

"Well, you may be aware that the economy goes through a boom and bust cycle, and that cycle peaks about every seven to ten years. Knowing this means that when the times are good and you are making good profits, you should be tucking some away for the lean years that will come along. I have to say I am always amused when I see the media reporting with shock and wonder, that a downturn in the economy hits every seven to ten years, as if it were a surprise. It's like being surprised that Christmas has hit and they didn't know!"

"Yeah," he agreed. "I've noticed that they always seem shocked when the economy goes down the toilet, as if it's never happened before."

"That's right." I replied. "And that's why you have to be prepared for such things. You need to make your money in the good years so you can survive the lean years. And to do that you need to understand the principles of how to make a profit…"

What Is Profit?

"Let me ask you Joe," I said. "What is profit?"

"That's pretty simple," he answered. "It's the money you make from selling stuff, or in my case from cutting people's hair."

"Sorry to say this Joe, but that's only part of the story." I replied. "What you have described is not profit, but sales. Typically accountants would call this revenue. Some would call it income and others call it receipts or receivables. There are lots of different names for what you described, but technically it is not profit. For our purposes we'll call it sales or revenue"

"So what would you call profit then?" he asked.

"Look, there are a lot of definitions of what is or isn't profit. In accounting circles they also look at it on a profit and loss statement at different stages of the statement, which is useful for analysis. But for our purposes let's keep it real simple. Profit is the money left over from your sales revenue AFTER you take out all of your costs. To state it like an equation it would be:"

SALES - COSTS = PROFIT

"Well…yeah," he said. "That's what I meant. Of course you gotta take out your costs."

Smiling I said to him, "I know Joe, and I was pretty sure you knew that too, otherwise you wouldn't have been in business for as long as you have. But not every small business owner knows this. A lot of people think that the money they get from sales is theirs to keep and spend as they choose. Let me tell you about a guy I went to school with (true story)."

"This guy, we'll call him Charlie, (not his real name), and I went to secondary school together. After we graduated I lost track of him for about ten years. Then I heard about him through a mutual acquaintance who told me that Charlie had gone into the plumbing business. At the time, by all accounts Charlie had what appeared to be a thriving contracting business."

"I can see that," Joe said. "Those trades guys make good money, especially the contractors."

"That's right," I replied. "Charlie appeared to be doing well. He had something like forty-five vans on the road and had a number of major building contracts to provide all of their plumbing work. He also had the big house, expensive cars, a boat and all the trappings of success."

"Sounds like he was doing well for himself. But I guess there is more to the story or you wouldn't be telling me?" Joe said.

"It does, doesn't it?" I replied. "And yes, there is more. A year or so later I heard that Charlie's business had folded and he had filed for bankruptcy. The car, house, boat and all the vans and sub-contractors were gone."

"What happened?" Joe asked curiously.

"Exactly what I said before. He did not understand that the sales or revenues he received were not profit, and he spent up big before paying his bills." I said sadly. "His was a classic case of poor money management because he didn't understand how money in business works. He did not plan and set aside the money he needed to cover the bills and taxes and so his business fell down in a crashing heap!"

"Wow," Joe said. "How could he not know that? Surely everyone knows that you can't go and spend what you don't have, or rather what isn't yours to spend?"

"I'm sorry to say but there are a lot of people in business who don't realize this is an issue." I said. "Some get away with it for a while. Some use overdraft loans, credit cards and even their creditors money by not paying bills on time to try and get out of a tight money jam. But if they don't learn the lesson before it's too late, they wind up where Charlie wound up."

"Now, before we get into the Profitability Principles," I said, "We need to consider a higher level view of your business."

"What do you mean?" Joe asked me.

"Every business should have goals they want to reach, not just a profit goal, but a business goal." I told him. "So before thinking about profitability, you need to consider what your goals are, why you want more profit and what you plan to do with the extra money when/if you get it."

Goals

One of the key points that needs to be stressed here, and Joe had the right idea, is to identify why you might want extra profit in your business.

Sure, it's easy to say "I just want more money," and many large businesses quote 'shareholder return' as a goal, but how much do you need?

Making money for the sake of money is not a real goal, nor is it a satisfying end in and of itself. I'm sure there are a lot of people who would disagree with this, but in my experience I have never found anyone who was seeking money as an end in itself to be satisfied or happy. They simply don't know when enough is enough, and when they get a lot of money, they seem to only want more. The purpose of making money is not the money itself, but what you plan to do with the money.

That is why it is essential that you have business goals FIRST. If you have goals in place, then you can determine how much money you need to achieve those goals, and set your financial goals in the best way to get there.

Joe has goals. We saw earlier that he is hoping to get

enough money from his small business to pay for the weddings of his two daughters. This gives Joe a very specific reason for increasing his business profitability so that he can achieve what he needs to do personally.

He has also employed a new barber in an attempt to build his business. So from a business perspective he also has a goal to grow his business for the longer term.

Every business should have targets for profitability, and these need to be driven by the goals for the business. The profitability targets should flow from the goals, not the other way around. That is like putting the cart before the horse.

The reason a business wants to grow their profits should also be identified and communicated within the business. When people have a goal or understand the reason why more profit is needed beyond simply accumulating money, they are more likely to be motivated to work towards the business profitability goals to achieve the higher goals of the business.

Now, I am not going to tell you how to set goals. That is not the purpose of this book. There are plenty of books and courses that can take you through the process of setting goals and the steps to achieve them.

What I will say though, is that it is necessary that goals be set AND written down AND reviewed on a regular basis. It has been credibly proven in many studies that those people who do these things will vastly outperform those who do not. And unfortunately only about 3% of the population actually does develop written goals.

So before you continue in this book, may I recommend you stop and consider, "What are your goals for your business that you want to improve your profitability for?" Oh, and if your business is in serious financial trouble…then survival is an acceptable goal!

Which brings us to the first of the principles you need to understand to ensure this will not happen to you. So let's pick up the story again with Joe.

It's Not How Much You Get, It's How Much You Get To Keep

Joe is a clever guy and he picked up on what I was saying pretty quickly. But like many small business owners, he had never had any background in accounting. He was pretty good at running his business and he always paid his bills. But the formula for what a profit is and is not still wasn't quite clear to him.

Many small business owners struggle with this concept, thinking that the money they earn is all theirs. It's not. A certain amount belongs to their creditors, suppliers, employees and the taxation department as well as any other people who provide a service, product, infrastructure or a license to do business.

So I had to simplify this in terms Joe could easily grasp.

"Joe," I said, "I know you get what I am saying, but to make it easier to understand let me make this first principle clear. In a nutshell Principle No. 1 can be stated as:"

"It's not how much you get, it's how much you get to keep"

"Does that make more sense?" I asked.

"OK, yeah, I see what you are saying now. You're saying that I have to pay out a whole bunch of money for all kinds of things to operate my business, and all of this comes from the sales I make. So I only get to keep whatever is left over. Is that right?" Joe said.

"Spot on, Joe. Now you get the idea." I responded. "There are a lot of small businesses, and even a few larger ones that seem to forget this basic principle of business. If you get this wrong, then you're gonna go broke."

"It seems pretty straightforward now that you explained it," Joe said. "How come so many people get it wrong?"

"Look Joe, I could go into a whole lot of detail as to why this is so, but other people have done a better job of explaining this than me. I'm trying to keep it simple for you." I said.

I went on saying, "If you want to know some more, there are lots of books that explain different aspects of these things. In my opinion, one of the best is a book by Michael Gerber called, 'The E-Myth Revisited' (Publisher: Harper-Collins)"

"What does he have to say about it?" Joe asked curiously.

"I won't go into detail, but at the highest level he suggests every business must have three primary functions if they are to succeed. They are the Entrepreneur who creates the business and builds it through sales and marketing efforts. Then there is the Technician, who is the person that is the expert at doing the job, such as cutting hair in your case. Finally there is the Administrator, who does all the bookwork and ensures the accounts are kept up to date and all monies are properly accounted for." I replied.

"Yeah, I can see how they are important and necessary to running a business, but what if it's a one man show like my business?" Joe asked.

"Well that's the point of his book." I said. "No-one is usually good at all three. Most businesses open up where someone is good at one, or maybe even two of these things, but it is an extremely rare individual who can do all three well. In the case of small businesses, it is usually the Administrator function that is poorly done, and that is why so many small businesses fail for lack of adequate cash control. He goes into a whole lot of other information on how to deal with such skill shortfalls and I would recommend you read his book."

"OK." Joe asked. "So is it a failure of the administration part of my business that I am not making the money I want?"

"No, Joe. In your case there are other things that can be done. Although your administration skills could maybe use a little work, generally you are doing OK. It's probably more in the Entrepreneurial category that you need some polishing up." I told him.

"Alright then," he said. "I guess for me though, the most important thing now that I understand that you don't get to keep all the money that comes in, is how do I improve my profitability?"

"And that my friend is a very good question, and one that we will start to address now." I replied.

The See-Saw Is Better Than The Swing

"The second principle flows on directly from the formula we spoke about earlier." I told Joe. "The formula, as you will recall is:"

SALES - COSTS = PROFIT

"So, to put it simply, if you want to make a profit, or to make more profit, you need to increase sales or reduce costs." I told him.

"I can see that," said Joe, "I tried to do that by putting on the new guy, Julio, and adding another chair to the shop. But my profits didn't really go up much at all, at least not nearly as much as I hoped and needed."

"Did adding the extra chair and hiring Julio increase your sales?" I enquired.

"Well, yeah. I got a reasonable increase in customers and we were able to get through them quicker with two of us cutting. But the sales probably only increased fifty percent above what I was able to do myself. By the time I took out the extra costs to pay Julio his wages, maintenance on extra shears, scissors, blades and such, as well as the cost of the new chair, I wasn't really much further ahead." Joe cried.

"Did you try anything else to get some additional business?" I asked.

"Only the Tuesday promotions I mentioned where I gave people a discount. It built a bit of business on what was normally a quiet day, but I also noticed a few of my regulars coming in on Tuesdays as well to get the cheaper prices. So the effect overall was pretty small." Joe said.

"OK," I said. "The basis of this second principle is that

you need to be able to increase sales WITHOUT increasing costs. Alternatively, you could decrease costs WITHOUT affecting sales. But the best way to approach this is if you can both increase sales AND reduce costs at the SAME TIME! That's why I call the second principle:"

"The See-Saw is Better than the Swing"

"Huh?" Joe said puzzled, "Can you explain that to me?"

"Sure. When your kids were young, did you take them to the local playground?" I asked him.

"Well, yeah, sure I did." Joe said reminiscing. "We used to go down to the local park and the girls would play for hours on the roundabouts, swings, slides and see-saws. They had so much fun, but I have to say it was sometimes tough for me, trying keep tabs on the two little rascals."

"And that is basically what I am talking about here too." I said. "Probably the only time you could be sure they were under your control was when they both played together on the see-saw. The seesaw goes up and down but it needs two people on it to work best, as one end goes up while the other end goes down at the same time. But a swing goes either up or down consecutively. A swing doesn't swing up as it is going down or vice versa. And as a parent you could keep an eye on the two girls when they played together on the see-saw, but when one of them was on the swing you would be distracted trying to keep an eye out for where the other one was."

"That's pretty much how it was," Joe said. "And you're right, when they played together on the see-saw they were easy to keep tabs on and both had a ball at the same time as they went up and down together."

"And that is what I am talking about with your business too." I said, pulling Joe from his reminisces. "In your business you need to 'work the see-saw' of costs and revenues so that as your sales revenue increases, your costs go down at the same time, just like a see-saw."

"Oh, OK. I see what you are driving at now." Joe said. "In the case of the swing, it only goes one way. Which means for my business it would be costs going down but no revenue increase, or sales going up but no costs falling. Is that bad though?"

"No it's not bad. It's a good thing if you can increase sales OR reduce costs, like a swing going back and forth. But it is much better if you can do both at the same time, like a see-saw going up and down." I told him.

"In your case, Joe, you increased your sales, but also increased your costs. So there was no appreciable change in your profit position." I said. "And it's not just small businesses that fall into this trap. Let me tell you a story about a BIG business that had this same problem (true story)."

"Some years ago when I was working for an industrial manufacturing company, I was chatting with the CEO. We got to talking about the retail arm of the business and he told me that the retail businesses were generating about $100 million in sales."

"Wow!" Joe said. "I wish I could get a piece of that action!" he chuckled.

"Yeah, well the only problem was that the CEO said the retail arm of the business cost about $100 million a year to operate and maintain after buying stock, paying wages, rent, utilities and so on. So how much profit was he making?"

"Zero!" Joe said. "So are you saying that with all that money they weren't actually getting to keep any?"

"That's right," I replied. "A huge amount of energy and effort went into stocking, resourcing and maintaining a segment of the business that was generating virtually no profit."

"Why didn't he just sell off the retail arm? Or maybe franchise it off?" Joe wondered aloud.

"I asked him the same question, and he had a good answer that is worth thinking about and remembering. The retail arm sold mainly industrial products that were aligned to and supported the company's manufactured goods. The company made most of its money through the distribution of their manufactured goods to other businesses. He told me that although the retail arm did not make any money, it did provide a free channel to market for the manufactured goods where they made the real profits."

"I see," Joe said. "It's not always as simple as it may seem at face value."

"No it isn't." I replied. "But the principle is the same regardless. If you want to make a profit you need to increase sales and reduce costs, preferably at the same time. In that industrial business they were trying to do that with the retail arm as well so they could contribute something extra to the bottom line."

"While we are talking about costs, I want to mention two types of costs that businesses speak about, without making it too complex. Accountants can refer to a lot of different types of costs, but for our purposes let's just keep it simple with two primary types.

The first set of costs is the direct costs that arise from the operation of the business to manufacture or retail their products. In a manufacturing business it might include raw materials, power, labor and so on that are used to produce the goods they are planning to sell. In a retail operation it would be the cost to buy the products they sell from their suppliers. Collectively these are typically called 'Cost of Goods Sold' (COGS) because they reflect the direct costs associated with manufacturing or acquiring the products the business sells." I explained.

"OK. So we will refer to these as cost of goods sold?" Joe asked.

"Yes, that's right. These are the costs that are directly impacted and will go up or down as sales volumes increase or decrease. They are directly related to the sales of items. The rest of the costs are the expenses incurred to run the business that do not fluctuate with sales. They include stuff like renting premises, stationery, depreciation, amortization, interest, distribution costs, staff salaries, electricity, tea and coffee and so on where these things are not part of the inventory for sale or used to directly produce things for sale. For the sake of simplicity let's call the first category COSTS and this second group we'll call EXPENSES."

"OK. I see now what you are saying." Joe said. "I need to get my costs and expenses down while I am increasing the sales through my shop if I want to get my profits up. So which is better? Is it better to focus on sales or costs to get the best effect?"

"Whoa there!" I said. "We're coming to that. But for now, why don't you go and look at your business again to see what you can do to improve your situation, given what you now know?"

"Good idea. I need to think about this some more. Can we get together again next week to discuss what I have come up with and to look at the next steps?" Joe asked.

"Sure. Let's do that. Besides, it's getting late and I think we both need to sleep on this before moving forward." I replied. "See you next week Joe," I said as I stood and started off home.

Not Every Dollar Is Equal

The following week I headed off to Joe's place wondering how he was doing. Had he thought about the things we had discussed? Was he ready to get into the real nitty-gritty of what was needed to improve his business profitability?

As I was about to knock on his door, the door flew open and a beaming Joe stood there.

"Come in, come in, my friend," he said smiling.

"You sound happy, Joe" I said to him grinning in return.

"I'm pleased to see you. I feel as though I'm just beginning to have my eyes opened to see what my business is about and what I need to do to improve it." Joe responded happily. "I feel as though there is a good future ahead and I can't wait to see what you have to show me this week."

"So, did you think over the things we spoke about last time?" I asked him.

"Indeed I did. I can see now that the money I get from cutting hair and selling hair products is not profit. That money represents sales revenues, from which I have to pay out all of my costs and expenses. I needed to learn that the money I get as revenue is not all mine to keep. I have to treat it as if I am a steward, making sure there is sufficient to pay all of the people and organizations I owe money to in order to keep the business running."

"That's right Joe. In fact the concept of being a steward is a good one too. A steward has control of all the business, but does not own it. The principle here is 'It's not how much you get, it's how much you get to keep,' and so like a steward, you don't get to keep anything until all the rest of the accounts have been dealt with." I reiterated for him.

"Exactly! Joe said. "And then when I understood that principle, I thought about the second one, 'The see-saw is better than the swing' which basically means, 'to make money you need to increase sales and decrease costs at the same time.' That was a tough one for me because I had worked to increase my sales, but unfortunately my costs went up in proportion, so I was really no better off. I was on the swing, not the see-saw!"

"Good analogy Joe, and that's why you need to work at doing BOTH cost reduction and revenue increase. So today let's look at another principle that will help you to do exactly that." I said.

"OK," Joe said. "Let's get to it!"

"Right. So today the principle I want to discuss with you is this…" I said.

"Not Every Dollar Is Equal"

"Huh?!?" Joe exclaimed. "Isn't a dollar just a dollar? Isn't a dollar always worth a dollar?"

"I know it's a little puzzling, but bear with me and I'll show you what I mean." I said to him.

"What I am talking about here is the impact of a dollar on your profit line. Remember last week we talked about sales, costs and expenses?"

"Yeah. Sales are the revenue we get by selling goods or delivering services. And we decided to call the costs of goods sold associated with manufacturing or purchasing goods for sale 'COSTS' and all the non-direct costs we said we would call 'EXPENSES.'" He said.

"That's right. In order to understand this principle that 'not every dollar is equal,' we need to understand the distinctions between these things." I replied.

"So how is a dollar of costs, revenue or expenses different from one another?" Joe asked. "Isn't a dollar still a dollar, regardless of what it is used for?"

"Well, a dollar is a dollar. But it's how much that dollar contributes to the bottom line that makes the difference." I explained. "Let me give you an example by drawing up a really simple profit and loss statement."

Qty Sold	100	
Cost/Unit	$7	
Selling Price/Unit	$10	
	$	% of Sales
Sales	$1,000	100%
less Costs	$700	70%
Gross Profit	$300	30%
less Expenses	$200	
Net Profit	$100	10%

Figure 1

"In this example we have a business that during a period of time, for our purposes a month, sold 100 units of product. It cost them seven dollars per unit to manufacture or procure this product (direct costs or cost of goods sold), and they sold each unit for ten dollars. So when you multiply the selling price by the units sold, we see they made $1,000 in sales revenue." I explained.

"Yeah...I can see that," Joe said. "But as we said before, this is 'What they got' but it's not 'what they get to keep'" Joe said. "They have to take out their costs and expenses before they get to keep anything," he said.

"That's right. And we can see from the numbers above that the costs to make or acquire the products were seven dollars per unit. If we multiply that by the number of units sold, our cost of goods sold is $700. So the Gross Profit is only $300, but it doesn't end there because we need to take out the non-direct expenses incurred during the month, which totaled $200. So they only get to keep 10% of the value of the sales, or one hundred dollars." I explained.

"But isn't this all just dollars?" Joe asked puzzled.

"Not when you think about the contribution to the bottom line." I told him. "Looking at this, we can see that for every dollar of sales, each dollar contributed only 10% or ten cents to the bottom line. So in this case a dollar of sales is only worth ten cents of profit."

"Oh, OK. I get that now." Joe said. "But how does this help me?" he asked.

"Well, when we understand these relationships at each level of the profit and loss statement, we can see that if we can tweak one of these levels it will have a different impact on the bottom line." I replied.

"Now let's say that this imaginary business managed to increase their sales VOLUME and they sold an additional 20 units that month." I said. "Then the profit and loss statement would look like this."

Qty Sold	120	
Cost/Unit	$7	
Selling Price/Unit	$10	

	$	% of Sales
Sales	$1,200	100%
less Costs	$840	70%
Gross Profit	$360	30%
less Expenses	$200	
Net Profit	$160	13%

Figure 2

"This time we see that every dollar of sales now contributes 13% to the bottom line. They received an extra $200 in sales revenue, but only an extra $60 in profit on the bottom line. So in relation to the overall sales, a dollar is now worth thirteen cents if they manage to sell more. The reason it goes up is because the non-direct costs or expenses are a much smaller proportion of the overall picture. To get a better idea, in this case we should look at the Gross Profit line where we see that the ratio of gross profit to sales has not changed. It's still 30% of sales." I said to Joe.

"At the Gross Profit level we only got an additional $60 in spite of selling 25% more products, and because the expenses don't change, all of that sixty dollars flows through to the bottom line." I explained.

"Yes I can see that. And this explains why I didn't make a whole lot of money when I put the new barber on. I increased my sales volume (haircuts), but also increased my overall costs. So the ratios didn't improve and I didn't end up making a whole lot more money." He said, beginning to understand.

"That's right, Joe, although your situation is a little different being a service business. There aren't really a lot of costs of goods sold in your line of work. So most of the increase in costs was in your expenses but with essentially the same effect." I explained. "What we learn from this is that for a manufacturing or retail business: *'A dollar in sales VOLUME increase is only worth the difference between the price per unit less the cost per unit, which is always going to be much less than a dollar.'*"

"OK. I can see that. So what comes next?" he asked.

"If we go back to our imaginary business, and look at the impact of reducing costs, we see a significant change. Lets see what happens if the business can reduce their manufacturing costs or procurement costs from seven dollars per unit down to six dollars per unit, and we'll go back to them selling only 100 units in the month." I said.

		% of Sales
Qty Sold	100	
Cost/Unit	$6	
Selling Price/Unit	$10	
	$	% of Sales
Sales	$1,000	100%
less Costs	$600	60%
Gross Profit	$400	40%
less Expenses	$200	
Net Profit	$200	20%

Figure 3

"Now we see a big change in profitability. Our Gross Profit has gone up a third from 30% to 40% giving us an extra one hundred dollars of gross profit. And again, because expenses don't change, all of that additional money goes into our pockets on the bottom line. Our profitability has doubled from $100 originally to $200 now." I said.

"Wow! That's a pretty big change!" Joe exclaimed.

"It is, but it's also hard work to try and find a way to reduce costs significantly. Most businesses have some fat in them that can be cut out, and most bigger businesses are constantly looking for ways to cut their costs, knowing that every dollar they can take out of their costs is worth a dollar on the bottom line." I said.

"Oh, I get it now," Joe said. "If we increase sales volume as we did in the previous example, every dollar that we got from increased sales was only worth an additional thirty cents of Gross Profit. But every dollar of reduction in costs or expenses is worth a full dollar at both the Gross Profit and Net Profit lines. And that's why you say not every dollar is equal!" Joe exclaimed with excitement.

"Now you've got it," I said. "So you can now see why it's important to keep costs down because: *'A dollar reduction in costs cut is worth a dollar of profit in your pocket.'*"

"But we also have another option that we can take on the sales revenue line. Let's say for instance that this same imaginary business was to increase their prices by one dollar, from $10 per unit to $11 per unit." I said. "And for the sake of comparison we'll go back to the original 100 units sold with a cost of seven dollars per unit."

	$	% of Sales
Qty Sold	100	
Cost/Unit	$7	
Selling Price/Unit	$11	
Sales	$1,100	100%
less Costs	$700	64%
Gross Profit	$400	36%
less Expenses	$200	
Net Profit	$200	18%

Figure 4

"Yes I see what is happening here," Joe said. "They still sold the same volume of units, but got a better price, picking up an extra one hundred dollars in sales revenue."

"Yes, that's right, Joe" I said. "And because the change was only in the pricing of each unit, there was no additional increase in the costs of production or procurement. So the whole one hundred dollars of the increase flowed through to the bottom line. Just like the reduction in costs in our previous example, *'A dollar increase in price is worth a dollar increase in profit.'* Now finally, if we look back at the second principle, 'The see-saw is better than the swing,' which means…"

"I know, I know, 'To make money you need to increase sales and decrease costs at the same time,'" Joe said in excitement.

"Yes, that's the one. Let's just take a look at the original scenario one more time where this imaginary organization did that. We'll leave the volumes as they were at one hundred units sold, but increase the selling price per unit from ten dollars to eleven dollars, and decrease the cost of goods sold from seven dollars to six dollars." I said.

Qty Sold	100	
Cost/Unit	$6	
Selling Price/Unit	$11	

	$	% of Sales
Sales	$1,100	100%
less Costs	$600	55%
Gross Profit	$500	45%
less Expenses	$200	
Net Profit	$300	27%

Figure 5

"Wow! What a difference this makes!" Joe said.

"Yes it does. If we look at the Gross Profit line we can see that it has increased from 30% originally to 45%. And more importantly, at the bottom line we are now getting to keep twenty-seven cents in the dollar instead of just ten cents." I said.

"This is incredible!" Joe exclaimed. "I just didn't realize the impact such changes could make and how I could benefit from it. You are absolutely right...not every dollar IS equal when it comes to the impact it has on the bottom line."

"Exactly! Every dollar of price increase and every dollar of cost reduction are worth a dollar on the bottom line. But a dollar in sales VOLUME increase is only worth the difference between the price per unit less the cost per unit, which is always going to be much less than a dollar." I summarized. "But if you do get sales volume increases as well as price increases and cost reductions, then you also pick up additional revenue anyway."

"I think this has given you enough to think about for this week, Joe." I said. "What say I let you mull this over and I'll come back next week and we can chat some more after you absorb it a little?"

"That sounds like a good idea. My head right now is bursting with all of this stuff. I'm just amazed at the simplicity of it and that I hadn't realized these relationships before!" Joe said.

"OK. I'll let you work on this and I'll see you next week. I hope this is helping you see your business a little differently!" I said as I stood to leave.

"It sure is," Joe said. "I'll see you next week."

The Power Of One Dollar

When Joe and I got together again the following week, his enthusiasm had softened a little. He had been hard at work looking at his business and trying to work out how he could apply the first three principles in order to improve his profitability. But he found it hard going and he hit a wall early on.

As I entered his home, he greeted me with this information saying, "Hi Johnny! I've been looking at the three principles so far and I can see how they could work in some businesses, but I don't know if they will work in mine." Joe said.

"Why is that, Joe?" I asked.

"Well, most of the change we saw in the businesses you described last time were to do with changes in costs of goods sold or price increases. I don't have much, if any, direct costs because all I do is cut hair." Joe said.

"That's right. Yours is a service business and with most service businesses you do not manufacture products for stock or buy in products for resale. In your case the only things that would fit the costs of goods sold are the hair products you sell, which are only a small proportion of your total revenue stream." I told him.

"So what do I do? I can't do anything significant to reduce costs of goods sold because there aren't any costs, which means all that is left is price increases." Joe exclaimed.

"There is still the opportunity of looking at your indirect costs or expenses, though. You might consider renting a different shop at a lower rate or negotiating a better rate where you are. You could look at changing your utilities providers for better rates and so on." I told him. "Even large organizations are always looking to improve in these areas, and you can and should too." I told him.

"However, as you may have guessed, these things take time, Joe. If you want to improve your profit situation more quickly, you will need to look at the possibility of putting your prices up." I said.

"But I can't do that!" Joe said with horror. "My loyal customers might leave and go somewhere else if I were to do that, and then I'd be in a worse situation!"

"OK," I said. "I understand how you feel, but you also need to be a little pragmatic about this. Let's have a quick look at your business for a moment to see what your current situation is."

We chatted for a while about his business and I learned a little about his operation. The key points were:

Haircuts per hour	3
Working hours/month	387
Price/cut	$12
Downtime (Typical)	25%
Sales/mth	
- Haircuts	$10,449.00
- Hair Products	$850
Total Revenue/Mth	$11,299.00
Less COGS	$552.50
Gross Profit	$10,746.50
Expenses	
- Wages	$6,020
- Electricity	$200
- Water	$150
- Phone	$450
- Advertising	$300
- Rent	$2,580
- Depreciation	$200
- Miscellaneous	$700
Total Expenses	$10,600
Net Profit	$146.50

Figure 6

After drawing up a rough profit and loss for Joe's business

using the information he provided, it was easy to see that he would not get the profit increase he needed from reducing his cost of goods sold (COGS). There may be scope for reducing his other costs, but the largest of those were wages for both himself and his new barber, which was enabling him to grow the business.

I advised Joe of this and told him, "Based on this I think your best option for bottom line growth would be price increase."

"No, no, no…" Joe said. "That might upset my customers. Surely there is some other way?"

"Well…" I said, "Before we throw the idea out completely, let's look at what just a ONE DOLLAR increase in the price of your hair cuts might add to your bottom line. Think about it realistically for just a moment. Do you think your customers would balk that much at an increase of just ONE DOLLAR?"

"I don't suppose it can hurt to look, I guess," Joe conceded.

So I ran the same set of numbers with only one change. I lifted the price per haircut from twelve dollars to thirteen dollars, and these were the results:

Haircuts per hour	3
Working hours/month	387
Price/cut	$13
Downtime (Typical)	25%
Sales/mth	
- Haircuts	$11,319.75
- Hair Products	$850
Total Revenue/Mth	$12,169.75
Less COGS	$552.50
Gross Profit	$11,617.25
Expenses	
- Wages	$6,020
- Electricity	$200
- Water	$150
- Phone	$450
- Advertising	$300
- Rent	$2,580
- Depreciation	$200
- Miscellaneous	$700
Total Expenses	$10,600
Net Profit	$1,017.25

Figure 7

"Wow!" Joe exclaimed. "That is quite a big difference! If

I could get profit levels like that by just increasing my prices by one dollar it would be worth doing! I'd certainly be able to get the money I need to pay for my daughters weddings in the next year or two with that kind of money."

"And that is the point of the whole exercise, after all." I said. "But before you go blindly putting up your prices, you have to research your market. You are worried about getting pushback from your customers and the possibility they may go elsewhere. So let's examine those things for a minute."

"Tell me Joe, when did you last increase your prices?" I asked, knowing that it had been at least several years. I'd been getting my haircut by Joe for a few years and couldn't recall a price increase in all that time.

"Umm…I think it was about five years ago," he replied.

"And in that time has your rent gone up, and your phone, advertising, electricity and so on?" I enquired.

"Well, of course they have!" he scoffed. "Everything keeps going up…!"

"Except for your prices," I pointed out. "You have been absorbing all of these costs for the last five years to the point where you are running yourself short."

"Yeah, I suppose I have. But I'm just thinking of my customers," Joe said.

"What do your competitors charge for a haircut?" I asked.

"Umm…they vary a bit. Anywhere from thirteen to eighteen dollars at the high end, I think." Joe replied, considering this.

"OK," I said, "Let's just consider these few things for a moment. It sounds as though you are at the low end of the haircut market when it comes to price, so the likelihood of a mass exodus if you were to increase your prices is pretty small. Also your customers will understand that the cost of doing business is quite high because, as you say, 'Everything is going up!' It sounds very much to me as though you would be quite justified to increase your prices, and you probably wouldn't cop too much of a backlash. In fact if anyone did push back, you could always remind them that they have had the benefit of you absorbing costs for the last five years while everything else went up. Anyone who doesn't accept that argument probably wouldn't accept anything else either."

"OK, Johnny. You've convinced me that I need to increase my prices. But I'm still a bit worried about my regulars. I don't want to lose any business." Joe replied.

"What I'd suggest then is to advertise the new prices in advance so they can get used to the idea and then it won't be a shock. People can talk about it and come to terms with the changes before the prices change." I told him.

"OK," he said. "That sounds like a plan that could work."

"While we are thinking about this Joe, it leads us to the fourth principle for making a profit, which is…"

No Pain, No Gain

As he was thinking about the impact of even a small price increase, Joe asked me, "So, what is the fourth principle?"

"The fourth principles is:"

"No Pain, No Gain"

"Come on, Johnny," Joe laughed. "I cut hair! I'm not an Olympic athlete or a weightlifter! What do you mean by 'No Pain, No Gain?"

"It's really quite simple," I said. "If you want to increase your profits, then someone is going to have to pay for it. That's the PAIN, and the profit is the GAIN."

"So how does it work?" Joe asked.

"Every decision that you make to improve your profitability position will impact someone." I told Joe. "That's why you need to be cautious and consider the impact of your decisions."

"Gee, that sounds serious!" Joe said frowning.

"Yeah, I guess it is. But it's not as bad as I'm making it sound. Anyone who applies these principles needs to do so from a considered and thoughtful position. Sometimes it's better to apply one principle rather than another. At other times it is better to do it a different way. You just need to think it through before making any changes." I said.

"Why is that?" Joe wondered.

"It comes back to the basis of this principle. If there is going to be a gain, then there will be pain. Someone is going to feel the pain. The question for you is to decide who should feel the pain as you make your profitability decisions." I told him.

"OK." Joe said. "So explain this to me in a little more detail."

"Alright," I replied. "Let's look at a couple of different scenarios. Do you recall the second principle I gave you?"

Thinking for a moment, Joe replied saying, "Yes. It was, 'The see-saw is better than the swing,' which means to make a profit you need to increase sales revenue and reduce costs. Oh, and it's best if you can do both at the same time."

"Exactly right," I said. "So let's think about that statement. Let's say you choose to increase your revenue by increasing prices. Who bears the PAIN in this situation?"

"Well…I guess it's the customer because he is going to have to pay more for a haircut." Joe said thoughtfully.

"Right again, Joe." I encouraged him. "The pain in this situation is going to be born by the customer."

"Well, I'm still a little nervous about putting up my prices and upsetting customers," Joe said. "But I understand it can be necessary to do that."

"Oh, absolutely!" I said. "In some cases it is not just necessary but is also the best way to address your profitability position. Look at your own situation for example."

"What do you mean?" he said.

"You are in the perfect place to increase prices." I responded. "The market price for haircuts in your area, based on how much your competitors charge, is a few dollars higher per cut than you charge. Also, you haven't increased your prices in some years and so it will not come as too great a shock to your customers, especially as they value your service."

"OK, I can see that." Joe replied.

"Now think about the pain YOU suffer because your profits are falling short." I challenged him.

"Yeah. I'll struggle to get the money to pay for my daughters' weddings and I may have to get into debt to do it. That will add more strain to me and the business might suffer because I am stressed." Joe mused.

"Do you think your pain might be greater than that of your customers?" I asked.

"In this case, I think so. In fact, since you opened my eyes to these things, I can see that if I do nothing then I could even go out of business in the next few years! Now THAT would be a major point of pain!" he grimaced.

"Exactly. And those are the kinds of things you need to consider when thinking about 'No Pain, No Gain.' You need to weigh up all of the options, positions and situations to identify where the greatest and least impact might be felt, and then make your decision." I explained.

"OK. But what if I chose to reduce my costs instead?" Joe asked.

"Well," I said, "If you reduce your costs, who bears the pain of your cost down decisions?"

"Umm…I guess I do?" Joe offered tentatively.

"Well, that's partly right. The other people who will bear the pain are people you pay money to, such as employees, creditors, suppliers and so on." I said. "The advantage of cost down decisions is that they are a lot easier to do because you are in control. You are the one who decides how much you are prepared to pay for products and services and you can change suppliers if you feel the service is not value for money. You can choose a cheaper place to rent, a less expensive hair products supplier or a different phone and electricity provider. And even if you are happy with the providers you already have, you can always go back to them as a loyal customer and ask for a better deal."

"Well that sounds OK, but it also seems like a lot of work." He said.

"It is a lot of work, but it won't impact your customers directly." I told him.

"Yes, I can see that," he said. "But it could impact them indirectly couldn't it?"

"Exactly right, Joe. If you go too far down the cost cutting path, you may begin to impact your capability. Let's say for example you put off the new guy, Julio, you hired to help out and so cut your wages costs. Would that impact your customers?" I asked.

"Of course it would!" Joe said. " We picked up a fair bit of extra business and I just wouldn't be able to handle it all by myself now! Customer service is critical in my business and to do that would destroy my service and I'd lose a lot of customers."

"And what if you moved to different premises? Let's say you found a much cheaper place in the rough end of town, for example." I said.

"Well, it would solve my workload issues!" Joe laughed. "A lot of people are too scared to venture down into the boon docks even during the daytime hours. I'd end up losing business. Not really what I want to do!"

"No." I grinned. "I'm pretty sure I'd be hesitant about going down there for a haircut myself!"

"Anyway," I added, "You can see how cost down decisions are not always easy to make and may not always be the best answer. Cutting costs will quickly improve profits, done properly. But when it starts to affect your capability to do business, then it can be as big a burden as trying to charge too much."

"Hmm," Joe thought out loud. "So is there anything else to this 'No Pain, No Gain' principle I should consider?"

"As a matter of fact there is." I said. "I mentioned before that any decision you make needs to consider who will bear the pain in order for you to get the gain. It's usually best if the pain falls to the one who will feel it least. To that end, there are a few ways that you can increase revenue or sales, one of which we covered here being to increase prices. But if you can't increase prices for some reason, then you need to consider increasing VOLUME. That is, how can you get more people through the door for haircuts?"

"I guess I could advertise more." Joe said. "I could maybe put out flyers around the neighbourhood offering a discount for new customers. Oh, and I heard recently that there's a new housing development about to be built just east of the shop. Maybe I could do something there too?"

"All great ideas Joe," I said, encouraging him. "And now think about who will suffer the pain for you to get the volume gain?"

"Well I suppose if I advertise I will be taking business away from my competitors, so I guess they will suffer the pain, won't they?" Joe said.

"Yes, that's right Joe. And being a competitive sort of guy, that's not a bad thing. Think about the people in the area who could get haircuts from you and/or your competitors as a big pie. What you would be doing is to try and get a bigger slice of that pie. So the competition will be the ones to suffer the pain. Be careful though…they will retaliate if they are any good at what they do, and if they see what you are doing!" I warned.

"Yeah, I guess so. It's never easy is it?" Joe said.

"Nope. There will always be pain and that pain can sometimes come back at you…especially when messing with the market." I said. "Although the other scenario about the new housing development is good. Rather than going head to head with your competition to get more of the pie, the pie just got bigger and you need to ensure you get as much of the growth in the size of the pie as possible." I told him. "If you can get all of the growth in the pie, then even though the competition may be affected, it will be less of an impact and they may not even see it coming. Growth in the size of the overall market is the best thing that can happen as it has the smallest impact on the players in the market, but remember, we don't control the increase in market size."

"OK then. All this talk of pies is making me hungry," Joe said with a laugh. "It sounds like it might be a good idea to go and chase the people in the new housing development when it gets built. I ought to start getting some flyers printed up and offer some decent discounts then to grab a bigger slice of the pie."

"Yes, it does. And I'm starting to get a little hungry myself." I told him. "How about we leave it there for now and we'll continue on next week. I think you have enough to digest, with or without pie for now."

"I think you're right," Joe said, laughing.

"Let's just quickly recap what we spoke about this week." I told Joe. "There are a few different scenarios that you need to consider if you want to improve your profitability, and in each situation you need to weigh up who will bear the pain so that you can get the gain."

"OK." Joe said.

"The four main scenarios can be built around where the gain will come from, and who will bear the pain." I told him. "They are:"

Market Growth - As a market expands there is little pain for anyone. However as you try to grab a larger share of the expanding market, it is the competition that will miss out.

Market Share - This is a direct grab for the customers already being served by a competitor, so it is the competition that bears the pain. But it requires some thought and caution, as they are sure to retaliate in some way.

Price Increase - Prices directly impact the hip pocket of your customers, so it is they who will bear the pain of increased prices.

Cost Reduction - Typically it is the suppliers, employees and creditors of the business that bear the pain of cost reductions. And if the reductions are too severe it can impact other parts of the business and customers by impacting on capability

"There is also a final aspect of costs that should be considered too, and it relates directly to your current situation, Joe," I said.

"What's that?" He asked.

"*Cost absorption.* As costs increase, you can choose to absorb the costs so as not to affect customers or suppliers. In that scenario though, YOU bear the pain and your profitability falls, and this is what you have been doing now for some years." I told him.

"Yes, I can see that now." Joe said. "And while it seemed like a good idea at the time, because I didn't want to impact my customers, it has not helped me achieve my goals, and how much worse would it be if I went out of business through doing this?"

"That's exactly right, which is why you need to think about these things. Oh, and by the way, don't get those flyers printed up until after our next session, because the flyers will relate directly to the last of the principles." I told him as I stood to leave.

"OK then. I'll see you next week." Joe said as we walked to his door.

The Discounting Dilemma

As I walked up to Joe's door the following week for what was to be our last session together, I considered the principles I had given him already. If he followed these principles I had no doubt that Joe would be able to achieve the profit improvements he needed to reach his goals.

The last of the principles I was to introduce him today, is a little more difficult, and one that is not easily understood by many businesses. I call it:

"The Discounting Dilemma"

I say this is not well understood in many businesses because so many businesses, both large and small have a tendency to discount, and often they discount heavily without understanding the effect it is having on their profit line. It is a dilemma because there are good reasons for discounting in certain circumstances, but it needs to be done for the right reasons.

I know from personal experience (true story) that I can walk into almost any business and get at least 10% to 15% off the shelf price of a product just by asking. In fact this is a ploy that my wife does VERY effectively, and she often gets as much as 30% or even 35% off retail price just by asking and haggling a bit. She lives by the philosophy: 'Never Pay Retail!'

And no, we are not talking about the market stalls found in many Chinese, South East Asian, Pacific Islands, Indian Sub-Continent or South American and similar countries where haggling over price is expected. We are talking about stores and businesses in countries like the USA, Australia, Canada, the United Kingdom, continental Europe and so on.

These thoughts were going through my mind as I walked

up and knocked on Joe's door that evening.

"Hi there, Johnny!" Joe exclaimed happily as he opened his door. "Come on in!"

"Hi Joe," I replied. "Good to see you. I expect we will finish our sessions tonight."

"Well, I'm both happy and sad to hear that," Joe said. "I have really picked up a lot and I have started applying these principles in my business. I took your advice and have notified my customers that I am increasing my prices…just a little, so the customers are not put off. Would you believe some of them even said, 'Well it's about time. Don't know how you managed to keep going with everything else going up!'" he laughed. "And even with the price rises, my haircuts are still much better value than my competition, so I don't think there will be any customer losses at all."

"I'm glad to hear that, Joe." I replied enthusiastically. "Just keep an eye on what is going on so that you can be sure that Principle #1 is met, which is…"

"Hold on, hold on." Joe said. "I know what it is. 'It's not how much you get, it's how much you get to keep.'"

"Spot on, Joe. And provided you are careful you should be able to keep ALL of the additional revenue you get from the price increase." I explained.

"Anyway, tonight I want to tell you about the Fifth Principle. This is especially relevant to your business since you are planning to put out flyers to pick up new business when the new housing estate is built. You didn't go and get the flyers printed up yet, did you?" I asked him.

"No, not yet. I took your advice and decided to wait until after this session." Joe replied. "Besides, the housing estate has only just started selling land so there won't be any houses built or people moving in for at least a few months or more, so I still have plenty of time."

"Great!" I said. "In that case let's get into the last principle, which is 'The Discounting Dilemma.'"

"The Discounting Dilemma?" Joe said. "Seems pretty straightforward to me."

"Well, it is and it isn't. Discounting is a great tool to use to attract more business and to get a sale. But you also need to understand what is happening when you give a discount so you can use this tool most effectively." I told him.

"Let me ask this first, Joe." I said. "What happens when you offer someone a discount?"

"Umm…well I just reduce the price so they don't pay as much. I do it mainly when I need to get a sale and it helps keep the customers happy too!" Joe said.

"I'm sure the customers are happy not to have to pay as much. How much do you discount by in those one-off situations?" I enquired.

"Oh…it depends. About 10% to 15% usually, depending on the customer and what I feel will be necessary to get his business." Joe added.

"OK then. You made the point that the customers don't pay as much when you discount. Where does that money come from?" I asked more pointedly.

He thought for a moment and responded saying, "Well, it's all part of the sales process, so I guess it comes out of my sales revenue?"

"That's what most people think. It is a common belief that when you discount a sale, it is the sales revenue that is impacted. Now, while that is true, there is a MUCH bigger impact on your profit, and after all, it is only the profit, 'that you get to keep.'" I told him.

"OK." He said, "Can you explain that to me?"

"Sure. Let's go back and look at the sales and profit numbers we used in that imaginary business a few weeks ago, just to keep it simple. OK?" I said.

"No worries, Johnny. It's a lot easier to understand with a few numbers." Joe said.

"OK. These were the original numbers, showing the sales, costs, expenses and profits." I told him.

"Yep. I remember these numbers." Joe said.

Qty Sold	100	
Cost/Unit	$7	
Selling Price/Unit	$10	
	$	% of Sales
Sales	$1,000	100%
less Costs	$700	70%
Gross Profit	$300	30%
less Expenses	$200	
Net Profit	$100	10%

Figure 8

"Now let's assume that the business manager decided to give his customers a 10% discount because he is worried about a new competitor on the block. Look at what happens to the numbers." I told him.

```
         Qty Sold    100
         Cost/Unit   $7
   Selling Price/Unit $9.00

                        $      % of Sales
             Sales    $900       100%
         less Costs   $700        78%
         Gross Profit $200        22%

         less Expenses $200
         Net Profit    $0          0%
```

Figure 9

"Can you see the impact of this decision, Joe?" I said

"Wow! He went from making a 10% net profit to zero!" Joe exclaimed.

"That's right. And this is the first part of the discounting dilemma." I said.

"Every Dollar Discounted is a Dollar Off Your Profit"

"I have to tell you Joe, that I can go into almost any

business and get a discounted price by 10% to 15% just by asking for it. They seem to think that a 10% reduction in the sales price is a minimal impact decision, and it is often left to counter staff. For some reason there seems to be a mental block where they think that 10% off the selling price is also only 10% off their profit too." I told him. "But as you can see in the example above, a 10% reduction in the selling price actually represented a 100% reduction in profit. They would have only broken even that month, if this were a real business. And if they gave 15% off it would have been a 106% reduction in profit, or a 6% LOSS!"

"I had no idea…" Joe said in shock. "Such a small discount can have such a dramatic impact? Who would have guessed!"?

"That's right, Joe." I said. "Discounting is basically another way of looking at the 3rd Principle, which is 'Not every dollar is equal.' In this case a dollar discounted off the sales price, in percentage terms has a much greater impact on the bottom line net profit."

"It's not all bad news, but you need to be aware of this because whatever percentage you discount the selling price by, will not be the same percentage off your profit. It will be greatly magnified by the time the price reduction hits your bottom line." I told him. "As an example, let's look at your business using the numbers you gave me, and let's assume you offered a 5% discount to all of your customers."

"OK, this should be pretty interesting. I'm dying to see what that impact might be." Joe said, with a hint of trepidation.

Haircuts per hour	3	
Working hours/month	387	
Price/cut (5% discount)	$11.40	
Downtime (Typical)	25%	
Sales/mth		% of Sales
- Haircuts	$9,926.55	
- Hair Products	$850	
Total Revenue/Mth	$10,776.55	100%
Less COGS	$552.50	
Gross Profit	$10,224.05	95%
Expenses		
- Wages	$6,020	
- Electricity	$200	
- Water	$150	
- Phone	$450	
- Advertising	$300	
- Rent	$2,580	
- Depreciation	$200	
- Miscellaneous	$700	
Total Expenses	$10,600	
Net Profit	-$375.95	-3%

Figure 10

"Seriously!" Joe said in horror. "I would actually lose

Not Every Dollar Is Equal

money by just offering 5% off the price of all my cuts!"

"That's right Joe," I told him. "But remember this is an unrealistic situation because you are not going to offer EVERY customer a discount."

"No, I know that," Joe said. "But if I look at this a bit deeper, I sometimes give people 10% or 15% discount, and so that would make it even worse. If I gave 10% to half of my customers it would be the same as giving 5% to all of them and so I would end up making a loss. And if I gave only 15% to one third of my customers, the same situation would apply." Joe said in shock.

"The reason why it is so bad is that your current profitability position is not great. If you were making heaps of profit, you wouldn't have the losses shown above. But since your profits are a quite low currently, it would be wise to not discount at all if possible."

"I can see that now. And I have been discounting on Tuesdays to try and get some more business, but all it has really done is moved a lot of my regulars to Tuesdays to get the cheaper prices." Joe said, horrified. "Gee! I really shot myself in the foot with this, didn't I!"

"Only because you didn't realize the impact of discounting." I told him, trying to let him off the hook a little. "I'm sure you can clearly see now the impact of a small discount and how a small discount off the sales revenue line can be greatly magnified by the time it hits the net profit line. In your example, the tiny 5% discount off sales revenue became a massive 103% off your profits, or a 3% loss, and no business can sustain that for long."

"Whew! OK then," Joe exclaimed. "So are you saying that I should never discount my prices?"

"No, not at all, Joe. I'm not saying that you should not

discount. What I am saying is that you need to understand the impact of discounting and how it affects your bottom line profits." I said. "This principle is called the 'Discounting Dilemma' and it is a dilemma for good reason."

"There are times when it is appropriate to offer a discount, and you had the right idea about it with your cheap Tuesdays." I told him.

"How do you mean? Wasn't I just cutting into my profits by doing that?" Joe asked confused.

"Yes you were when your existing customers took up the offer. But you did gain some new business, didn't you?" I asked.

"I did get a few new customers." Joe replied.

"And that was the whole point of why you discounted on Tuesdays. To get some more customers and to pick up a little on what you said was a slow day." I added. "The point of discounting and the answer to the dilemma is that it is OK to discount if you are seeking to gain more volume. That is, you can discount if you are trying to get more new customers."

"So it's OK to offer discounts to get new business, but I shouldn't discount existing business?" He asked.

"Basically that's correct." I told him. "Although even then you might need to discount existing customers on occasions. Let's say for instance you get a new competitor, or an existing competitor tries to aggressively take away your customers. You might need to discount to retain your business, unless there is some other value you can add that the competition can't or doesn't do. Value adding is better because it won't eat into your profits and might give you a new revenue stream, but if that isn't successful, discounting might be necessary."

"My point with this final principle is that whatever you do, discounting needs to be a well thought out and well considered approach. It should not be taken lightly, and certainly not as lightly as many businesses take it. The profit impact is quite significant, as you saw above." I told him.

"So let's now look at your plan for growth, Joe." I said. "You are planning to offer a discount for new customers in the new estate that is opening up. What sort of discount did you have in mind?"

"I was thinking maybe an introductory offer of 15%, but now I wonder if that is too high?" Joe said.

"Well, let's use that number and see what the impact on your business might be. How much new business do you think you could get?" I asked him.

"Gee, I don't really know. That's sort of a 'How long is a piece of string' question." Joe mused, thinking out loud as he continued on. "I know the housing estate will have around 600 new homes when completed, and it will mostly house younger families. If we said there were two parents and two kids on average that would be 2,400 heads of hair. I only do men's and boy's haircuts so assume half of that number, or 1200 heads that would need haircuts. Most guys around here seem to get their hair cut on average every six weeks, so that would be 200 cuts a week. Now I know I won't get all of the business, and besides I couldn't currently handle that many extra cuts, even with Julio. Based on our current available downtime we could handle about 70 additional cuts a week, which I think is probably reasonable. If it gets too busy I might have to bring on a part-timer to fill the gap."

"OK. Given we don't really know what might happen, let's make a wild assumption that you will pick up the additional 70 cuts a week at a 15% discount. And let's assume they all come through in the first month." I said.

"And yes, it's probably unrealistic because people will only slowly move into the estate as houses are built and it probably won't be all complete for well over a year. But for the sake of this exercise, let's assume the estate is nearly complete before you run your promotion, and they all come in the same month to get a haircut at the reduced rate. This is what the numbers will look like."

Haircuts per hour	3
Working hours/month	387
Price/cut	$12
Downtime (Typical)	0%
# normal price cuts	871
# discounted cuts (15%)	290

Sales/mth	
- Haircuts (normal rate)	$10,449.00
- Haircuts (15% disc. rate)	$2,958.00
- Hair Products	$850
Total Revenue/Mth	$14,257.00
Less COGS	$552.50
Gross Profit	$13,704.50
Expenses	
- Wages	$6,020
- Electricity	$200
- Water	$150
- Phone	$450
- Advertising	$300
- Rent	$2,580
- Depreciation	$200
- Miscellaneous	$700
Total Expenses	$10,600
Net Profit	$3,104.50

Figure 11

"The effect of discounting for volume growth to gain NEW business is not as dramatic as the impact of discounting existing customers. It is especially relevant in a service industry such as yours Joe, because there is no real cost of goods sold. Rather, you are simply getting more dollars for the hours where you previously got none. And if these new customers like your work and you can retain them as regulars, then the future income from those new customers will be at your normal rate, not the discounted rate, which will add to your profits even further." I told him. "Plus, by the time this all takes place you should have new pricing in place for the existing customers which will add even more to your profit line."

"I can see now why it is a dilemma." Joe said, "Discounting needs to be thought about and not just applied willy-nilly, because it can do serious damage to my profit line."

"Yes, and if you happened to be in a retail or manufacturing business, then you would need to consider the impact of the Cost of Goods Sold line more closely." I told him. "When those types of businesses are picking up additional volume, they should never sell or discount below the Cost of Good Sold rate, because then they are going to lose money on every additional sale and cut into the profits made on products sold at the normal retail price." I said. "Remember that every dollar discounted flows directly through to the bottom line profit, and if you are in retail or manufacturing and you discount below the Cost of Goods Sold, then you are taking away profit from the business."

"Thanks for this insight, Johnny," Joe said. "It has been quite a journey and I have learned a lot from these principles that will help me achieve my business and personal goals."

Summary

"There's one last thing we ought to do before we call it a day, Joe." I said to him.

"What's that?" he asked me.

"I just want to summarize the principles and what we have discussed briefly over these past few sessions." I told him.

"Yeah…it would be good to have a bit of a summary." Joe said. "It would help me going forward."

"OK then, let's look at what we have covered." I said.

"First, we looked at why businesses go bust, and although there can be countless reasons, many of them fail due to a lack of good money management. Many businesses, especially small businesses, fail to grasp the implications of their actions on the profitability of their business. We looked at what profit is and is not and identified that: SALES REVENUE – COSTS = PROFIT"

"Yep. I got that. Especially after our discussions I can see how confusing it can be. In fact I now believe I probably got through more by good luck than good management because I didn't really understand this stuff either." Joe replied.

"That's right Joe, although you weren't too bad because you are naturally cautious with money." I said. "However knowing what you know now you can plan better and price better."

"The second thing we looked at was to consider the goals of the business. Profit alone should not be the goal of any business. The key should be what you plan to do with the profits you make, and identifying how much you need to make to achieve your business and personal goals. You have some goals that you need the money for and that is what you are working towards, which is great." I told him.

"Yeah I can see now that the goals I have are what will or should drive my business decisions, especially as regards profitability." He acknowledged.

"The next thing we looked at was the first of the five principles: 'It's not how much you get, it's how much you get to keep.' This is a direct link back to the definition of what profit is. You do not get to keep all the money earned from your sales and/or revenue streams. What you get to keep is the money left AFTER paying out all of your costs and expenses from the revenue streams."

"That made good sense to me." Joe said. "You can't or shouldn't spend money that technically isn't yours to spend."

"That's right." I told him. "So the next important thing to do for any business is to consider the second principle that leads directly on from the first one, which is: 'The see-saw is better than the swing.' And the meaning of this was: 'To make money you need to increase sales and decrease costs at the same time.' Sometimes you can't do both, but it is important to consider how this might be achieved. If we can increase sales revenues while we decrease our costs, then we can greatly multiply our profits."

"That's right," Joe said. "But there are ways that are better than others to achieve both ends."

"Yes. And this brings us to the third principle: 'Not every dollar is equal.' When it comes to the impact on the profit line, a ONE DOLLAR reduction in COSTS, or a ONE DOLLAR increase in PRICE will flow directly into the net profit line. But a ONE DOLLAR increase in revenues or sales is reduced by the Cost of Goods Sold that is required to generate that sale. Thus, you only get a portion of the sales dollars flowing into the profit line. To put it bluntly, a DOLLAR increase in SALES is NOT a dollar increase in profit."

"That was a big lesson for me," Joe said. "It is one I intend to implement based on my knowledge now of the impact and the market."

"I agree, and that takes us to the fourth principle: 'No Pain, No Gain.'" I told him. "Any time you are going to try to improve your profitability, someone is going to have to pay for it. Someone is going to 'take the hit' so to speak. Someone will suffer the financial pain in order for you to get the profit gain. Depending on the approach you take it may be the customer, a competitor, or even your own business. Whatever happens, when there is a change occurring in the profitability of the business, there will be both pain and gain."

"I know that now," Joe said. "And I also know that by doing nothing, such as when my costs increase, then I suffer the pain for NO gain, and that really isn't a viable position to be in. I know also that I need to understand who is going to take the pain if I plan to change anything so that I don't cause problems to the wrong group of people and consequently upset my business"

"Exactly." I told him. "Doing nothing when the economic environment or the market environment changes can be a recipe for disaster, which is why it is essential to watch what is going on around you and make profitability decisions that will minimize the pain."

"And then we came to the fifth and final principle, which is: 'The Discounting Dilemma.'" I said.

"This was a big one for me." Joe replied. "I really had no idea how just a small change, a small discount, in the selling price could potentially have a massive impact on my business. It was a real eye-opener!"

"Yes it is, and given how easy it is to get discounts from almost all businesses, it is evident that many of them don't understand the issue either. But as I said, it is a dilemma because sometimes you do need to discount and sometimes it is the appropriate thing to do. My general rule of thumb is that unless you are getting more volume in your sales, then don't discount. Otherwise you are eating into your profits. Also, you should not discount in any business unless you have a solid grasp on your cost base and understand how the discounts will affect overall profitability. Discounting should be a considered decision, not an ad-hoc one left to counter staff."

"And that's about it, Joe" I added. "Hopefully you will get value out of this and it will help you achieve your business and profitability goals."

"It sure will, Johnny! I really appreciate you laying this out for me. This information has been a real boon and an eye-opener to me. I am now certain I can take the business to bigger and better things and achieve my goals." He said.

With that I took my leave. There are a whole lot more things Joe could learn to help him improve his understanding of his business, but this was enough to get him on the right path. I decided we would cover other things at a later time when he was ready to go to the next level.

I hope you too, will get some value and can see opportunities to improve your profitability through a better understanding of what is going on in your business as pricing, costing and profitability decisions are being made.

Printed in Great
Britain
by Amazon